Dysphagia Placement Workbook

Naomi Cocks and Celia Harding

J&R Press Ltd

Acknowledgements

We would like to thank all the students at City University London who completed dysphagia intensive placements and gave feedback on the workbook. We would especially like to thank all the clinical educators who have taken students on dysphagia intensive placements and also gave feedback on the workbook. In particular, we would like to thank Camille Paynter, who piloted the dysphagia placement, has aided in the roll-out of this placement model, gave feedback on earlier versions of this workbook and helped with proofreading. We would also like to thank Madeleine Pritchard and Natalie Hasson for proofreading earlier versions of this workbook.

About the Authors

Naomi Cocks is a senior lecturer, clinical tutor and clinical educator in the Department of Language and Communication Sciences at City University London. She lectures on dysphagia to pre-registration students and qualified speech and language therapists. Prior to becoming a lecturer, Naomi worked in Australia as a speech pathologist in a range of settings including acute, rehabilitation and community facilities. In these settings she assessed and managed clients with a range of swallowing difficulties and also supervised many students.

Celia Harding is a senior lecturer, clinical tutor and clinical educator in the Department of Language and Communication Sciences at City University, London. As a speech and language therapist she continues to practise at The Royal Free Hospital as part of the paediatric gastroenterology team. She teaches in the areas of learning disability, which includes augmentative and alternative communication and paediatric dysphagia both at pre-registration and post-registration level.

Contents

Welcome to students and newly-qualified therapists

Welcome to your Dysphagia Placement Workbook. This workbook is designed specifically for speech and language therapy students and newly-qualified therapists in order to prepare you for a clinical placement or new post that has a focus on dysphagia. It has also been designed to facilitate your learning whilst on this clinical placement or in this new post. It provides a structured learning approach for developing basic competencies in the field of dysphagia. The structure of this workbook means that specific tasks can become embedded within your own professional development plan in a progressive way.

The workbook was developed as part of a research project that ran at City University London in 2009–2010. This research project investigated the impact of a 5-day dysphagia placement on student confidence and knowledge. Qualitative feedback was collected about the workbook from clinical educators and students and it was modified in light of this feedback.

The workbook will help you – and your clinical educator or supervisor – to structure and plan your clinical time while on your dysphagia placement or in your new post. The activities in this workbook are designed so that you will get the most out of this placement.

Some of the activities relate specifically to clinical observation and clinical knowledge. Others are more focused around reflecting on the situation that you have been in. We feel that this combination of approaches is a positive method of maximising your learning and confidence in this area. You are encouraged to share your findings both with clinicians and with your peers.

At the back of this book you will find a checklist of activities. When you complete an activity, ask your clinical educator or supervisor to view the completed activity and sign the checklist to indicate that you have completed this activity. This page may be photocopied and given to your university or used in your professional development portfolio.

You are encouraged to do additional reading before and whilst on your placement. We have recommended some articles for each of the activities. However, we encourage you to read more about dysphagia by carrying out searches of relevant databases, e.g. PubMed, and reading articles from the journal *Dysphagia*. Your clinical educator or supervisor may also recommend additional reading to support your learning whilst on the placement.

In order to prepare yourself for a dysphagia placement, before its commencement you will need to complete the pre-placement learning activities in this workbook.

Naomi Cocks and Celia Harding
City University London

Welcome to clinical educators and supervisors

Welcome to the Dysphagia Placement Workbook. This workbook has been designed specifically to help you plan for and support the learning of speech and language therapy students on a clinical placement that focuses on dysphagia. It may also be used with newly-qualified speech and language therapists who have started a new post that has a dysphagia component.

The workbook was developed as part of a research project that ran at City University London in 2009–2010. This research investigated the changes in student confidence and knowledge after a 5-day 'dysphagia intensive' placement. The workbook was designed to help clinicians structure the 5-day placement and to promote consistency across placements. As part of the research project, qualitative feedback was collected about the workbook from clinical educators and students. This led to a number of changes being made to the workbook, including the inclusion of additional activities such as Fibreoptic Endoscopic Evaluation of Swallowing (FEES).

The activities in this workbook were carefully designed to ensure that students get the most out of this placement and will begin to develop basic competencies in dysphagia. The activities were inspired by teaching and learning research, the King's Dysphagia Schedule (Gascoigne & Marks, 2001) and competencies discussed in the Speech Pathology Australia's Dysphagia Position Paper (2004). For more information about the development of and rationales for these activities, and for additional activity ideas please refer to the accompanying book: Cocks, N. & Harding, C. (2011). *Developing Clinical Skills in Dysphagia: A guide for speech and language therapists* (London: J&R Press).

The accompanying book also contains additional materials to help support many of the activities in the workbook. Examples include:

- a DVD with videofluoroscopic swallowing studies that can be used in the activity on videofluoroscopic swallowing studies
- checklists to aid students in clinical writing and examples of clinical writing
- templates for case history taking

At the back of this book you will find a checklist of activities. When the student or a newly-qualified therapist has completed an activity, please view and give feedback on the completed activity and then sign the checklist to indicate that they have completed this activity. This page may be photocopied and given to the student's university or used in the newly-qualified therapist's professional development portfolio.

Please note that this workbook is designed to help and support students and newly-qualified therapists develop basic competencies in dysphagia. Completion of all activities in this book does not mean that the student or therapist is competent enough to work independently with clients with dysphagia.

The workbook was designed with both UK and Australian students and newly-qualified therapists in mind and therefore refers to relevant policies and guidelines within these countries at the time of print. For ease, the UK title 'speech and language therapist' has been used throughout the workbook as opposed to the Australian title 'speech pathologist'.

We hope you enjoy using these materials with speech and language therapy students and newly-qualified therapists within your work environment.

Naomi Cocks and Celia Harding
City University London

General notes

Pre-placement preparation for students

It is essential that, prior to this placement, you familiarise yourself with the standards of proficiency, risk management procedures and ethical issues. You should also ensure that you have an awareness and basic understanding of the relevant theory. This preparation will ensure that you get the most out of your placement experience and will help to minimise risk.

Standards of proficiency

It is essential that, prior to this placement, you refresh your knowledge about dysphagia in relation to good practice and basic competencies.

UK speech and language therapy students should refer to:

- Health Professions Council (2007). Standards of Proficiency: Speech and Language Therapists. London: HPC.
- RCSLT (2006). Communicating Quality 3: RCSLTs guidance on best practice in service organisation and provision. London: RCSLT.

Australian speech pathology students should refer to:

- Speech Pathology Australia (2001). Competency Based Occupational Standards (CBOS). Available on the Speech Pathology Australia web page: http://www.speechpathologyaustralia.org.au
- Speech Pathology Australia (2004). Dysphagia General: Position Paper (2004). Available on the Speech Pathology Australia web page: http://www.speechpathologyaustralia.org.au

Ethical issues

The following features are crucial aspects of any treatment plan involving clients with dysphagia (Beauchamp & Childress, 1994, cited in Winstock, 2005):

Beneficence You are acting in the best interests of the client and family based on your clinical assessment and judgement.

Non-malificence You should not consider a strategy that will cause greater harm, risk or problems for the client.

Autonomy You must respect the client's and the family's wishes; although sometimes these may clash with what you feel is the safest and most appropriate intervention for a client. This is why you need to constantly be in touch with the key members of the Multi-disciplinary Team (MDT) so that risk is continually re-appraised and minimised.

Justice Make sure that your service delivery is equitable.

Safety Above all, your intervention is about safety as well as maximising skills. It is about the identification of aspiration and choking risk, and reducing the risks where possible. You need to consider the following questions:

– Is the client's cough reflex safe?

– Is the client at risk of dehydration and/or malnutrition?

– Is the aspiration chronic, therefore leading the team to consider alternative feeding, or can the aspiration be managed by careful strategy management?

– Can texture modification provide opportunities for safe eating and drinking?

– Are the carers capable of carrying out your intervention plan?

– Do the nursing staff you work with need ongoing training?

Additional reading

Prior to starting placement or your new post, it is advised that you read the following:

- Huffman, N. & Owre, D. (2008). Ethical issues in providing services in schools to children with swallowing and feeding disorders. *Language, Speech & Hearing Services in Schools, 39,* 167–176.

- Wasson, K., Tate, H. & Hayes, C. (2001). Food refusal and dysphagia in older people with dementia: Ethical and practical issues. *International Journal of Palliative Nursing, 7(10),* 465–471.

- Winstock, A. (2005). *Eating and drinking difficulties in children: A guide for practitioners*. Milton Keynes: Speechmark.

Australian speech pathology students and newly-qualified therapists should refer to:

- Speech Pathology Australia (2010). Code of Ethics. Available on the Speech Pathology Australia web page: http://www.speechpathologyaustralia.org.au

UK speech and language therapy students and newly-qualified therapists should refer to:

- Royal College of Physicians and British Society of Gastroenterology (2010). *Oral feeding difficulties and dilemmas: A guide to practical care, particularly towards the end of life*. London: Royal College of Physicians of London. Available at: http://bookshop.rcplondon.ac.uk/contents/pub295-ca2ff0c8-85f7-48ee-b857-8fed6ccb2ad7.pdf
- Royal College of Speech and Language Therapy (2006). *Communicating Quality 3: RCSLTs guidance on best practice in service organisation and provision*. London: RCSLT.

Specific risk issues

1. Once a duty of care has commenced, it must be discharged in full. Negligence can be an act that causes harm. The speech and language therapist remains responsible for his/her own acts and omissions (refer to RCSLT and HPC, or SPA guidelines).

2. Intervention with clients with eating and drinking difficulties may be required at short notice, and therapists should ensure their availability to discharge their duty of care according to local guidelines. In many UK facilities this means that in-patient referrals will be seen within one to two days of receipt of referral and outpatients within two weeks of referral.

3. Given the potential life-threatening nature of eating and drinking difficulties, a speech and language therapist has a duty to do whatever is reasonably expected of them in those circumstances.

4. Speech and language therapists should follow local service health and safety guidelines. They should ensure that they are adequately prepared for such events and are familiar with emergency procedures and general safety procedures.

5. Speech and language therapists working with clients with eating and drinking difficulties should recognise their individual levels of competence, and seek second opinions as appropriate.

6. Speech and language therapists should be aware of the risks of radiation when carrying out a videofluoroscopic swallowing study.

7. Speech and language therapists may be working with vulnerable babies, children and adults. Consequently, they have a duty to safeguard the children under their care, and need to be familiar with child protection policies and procedures (e.g. in the UK The Children Act, 2004). Speech and language therapists should also be aware of policies and procedures relating to vulnerable adults (e.g. in the UK DoH: Safeguarding Vulnerable Adults: Regional Adult Protection Policy & Procedural Guidance, 2006).

> **On your first day of your dysphagia placement, you must check the service provider's requirements for risk management, infection control and choking management.**

Resources

Australian students should refer to the relevant state's Department of Child Protection for guidelines.

UK students should refer to:

- Department of Health, Social Services and Public Safety. (2006). Safeguarding Vulnerable Adults: Regional Adult Protection Policy & Procedural Guidance, 2006. http://www.nhssb.ni.nhs.uk/
- Children Act 2004, H.M.S.O. 2004. http://www.legislation.gov.uk/ukpga/2004/31/contents

Pre-placement quiz 1: Dysphagia knowledge self-assessment

This quiz needs to be completed before you begin your clinical experience within dysphagia. Completing these activities will enable you to consider key concepts relevant to dysphagia across paediatric and adult caseloads.

Note to clinical educator or supervisor. The answers to this quiz can be found in the accompanying book:

- Cocks, N. & Harding, C. (2012). *Developing clinical skills in dysphagia: A guide for speech and language therapists.* London: J&R Press Ltd.

Some suggested resources

- Arvedson, J.C. & Brodsky, L. (1993). *Paediatric swallowing and feeding: Assessment and management.* Albany: Singular Publishing Group
- Cichero, J. & Murdoch, B. (Eds) (2006). *Dysphagia: Foundation, theory and practice.* Chichester: John Wiley and Sons Ltd
- Groher, M. & Crary, M. (2010). *Dysphagia: Clinical management in adults and children.* Missouri: Mosby
- Daniels, S.D. & Huckabee, M.L. (2008). *Dysphagia following stroke.* Plural Publishing: San Diego
- Logemann, J.A. (1998). *Evaluation and treatment of swallowing disorders.* Austin: Pro-Ed Publishers
- Love, R. & Webb, W. (2001). *Neurology for the speech-language pathologist.* Oxford: Butterworth-Heinemann
- Winstock, A. (2005). *Eating and drinking difficulties in children: A guide for practitioners.* Milton Keynes: Speechmark

Instructions

This knowledge assessment is for you to reflect on your dysphagia knowledge so far. We recommend that first you try to do this quiz without referring to the texts listed above. Once you have checked your answers in the text and discussed them with your clinical educator, you may wish to reflect on which aspects you will need to focus on to consolidate your learning.

1. Fill in the following table indicating the general functions of each of these cranial nerves, the impact that damage to the nerve will have on swallowing and how you test the function of the nerve.

Cranial nerve	General function	Impact of damage on swallowing	How is the function of the nerve tested ?
V			
VII			
IX & X			
XII			

2. Write down how you would go about investigating cranial nerve function in (i) an infant; (ii) a child with complex physical and learning needs; and (iii) an adult with receptive aphasia.

....

....

....

....

....

....

....

....

....

....

....

....

....

....

....

....

....

....

....

....

....

....

....

....

3. Fill in the following table.

Oral phase disorders	Clinical signs:
	Observations you would expect when viewing VFSS/FEES:
	Possible causes:
Pharyngeal disorders	Clinical signs:
	Observations you would expect when viewing VFSS/FEES:
	Possible causes:
Aspiration	Clinical signs:
	Observations you would expect when viewing VFSS/FEES:

4. Describe the swallowing difficulties associated with a weak base of tongue.

....

....

....

....

....

....

....

5. What causes nasal regurgitation?

....

....

....

....

....

....

....

6. What is the function of the lips in swallowing?

....

....

....

....

....

....

....

....

7. What is the function of the epiglottis in swallowing?

....

....

....

....

....

....

....

....

....

....

....

....

8. What happens if the upper oesophageal sphincter does not open during swallowing?

....

....

....

....

....

....

....

....

....

....

....

9. This is a diagram of the adult anatomy. Write down three key
features as to how this DIFFERS from an infant's anatomy.

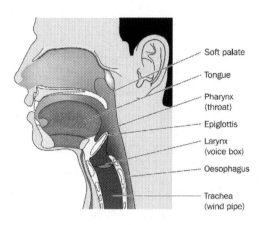

....

....

....

....

....

....

....

....

....

....

....

....

....

....

10. Describe what you would expect (i) an infant; (ii) a 6-month-old child; (iii) a 12-month-old child; (iv) an 18-month-old child; and (v) a 24-month-old child to be eating?

....

....

....

....

....

....

....

....

....

....

....

....

....

....

....

....

....

....

....

....

....

....

....

....

11. Describe a minimum of four key features within an adult or a paediatric population that would predispose you to consider that the client had aspiration.

....

....

....

....

....

....

....

....

....

....

....

12. Describe a non-instrumental dysphagia assessment that can be used for an adult or a child. Describe the key features that are observed and evaluated when using this assessment. It may be helpful to consider a commercially-available assessment, for example, the MASA: Mann Assessment of Swallowing Ability by Giselle Mann (2002), or the SOMA: Schedule of Oral Motor Assessment by Sheena Reilly et al. (2000).

....

....

....

....

....

....

13. What is a videofluoroscopic swallowing study, and what are the criteria for using this instrumental evaluation as an assessment tool?

....
....
....
....
....
....
....
....
....
....
....
....
....
....
....
....
....
....
....
....
....
....
....
....

14. Compare the following assessments: videofluoroscopic swallowing study and fibreoptic endoscopic evaluation of swallowing. What are two key advantages and disadvantages of each of these assessments?

....

....

....

....

....

....

....

....

....

....

....

....

....

....

....

....

....

....

....

....

....

....

15. Describe three management and/or therapy approaches that you have read about for an adult dysphagia caseload, or three management and/or therapy approaches for a paediatric caseload.

....

....

....

....

....

....

....

....

....

....

....

....

....

....

....

....

....

....

....

....

....

....

....

16. Some medications can have an impact on appetite and/or swallowing. Typically, such medications include anti-convulsants, analgesics, anti-depressants and tranquillisers. Carry out a search to investigate how medication can impact on a specific client group and write down your findings. Consider the side effects and the potential effect on the swallow. An example could be the anti-convulsant Phenytoin. This can cause nausea and vomiting, but can also contribute to poor oral motor control and uncoordinated swallowing.

....

....

....

....

....

....

....

....

....

....

....

....

....

....

....

....

....

....

Pre-placement quiz 2: Oral hygiene and aspiration pneumonia

Resources

- El-Solh, A., Pietrantoni, C., Bhat, A., Okada, M., Zambon, J., Aquilina, A. et al. (2004). Colonization of dental plaques: A reservoir of respiratory pathogens for hospital-acquired pneumonia in institutionalized elders. *Chest, 126(5)*, 1575–1582.

- Langmore, S., Terpenning, M., Schork, A., Chen, Y., Murray, J., Lopatin, D. et al. (1998). Predictors of aspiration pneumonia: How important is dysphagia. *Dysphagia, 13*, 69–81.

- Meguro, K., Yamagauchi, S., Doi, C., Nakamura, T., Sekizawa, K. and Sasaki, H. (1992). Prevention of respiratory infections in elderly bed-bound nursing home patients. *Tohoku Journal of Experimental Medicine, 167(2)*, 135–142.

- Pace, C.C. & McCullough, G.H. (2010). The association between oral microorgansims and aspiration pneumonia in the institutionalized elderly: Review and recommendations. *Dysphagia, 25(4)*, 307–322.

A self-directed oral hygiene learning package is also available online at: http://www.cetl.org.uk/learning/OHI_dysphagia/player.html

1. Why is oral hygiene an important consideration in the management of infants, children and adults with dysphagia?

....

....

....

....

....

....

....

....

....

....

....

....

....

2. What are some of the risk factors for aspiration pneumonia?

....

....

....

....

....

....

....

....

....

3. What do a healthy mouth and healthy gums look like?

....
....
....
....
....
....
....
....
....

4. Why are people who have disabilities, dementia and/or are nil by mouth at high risk of having poor oral hygiene?

....
....
....
....
....
....
....
....
....
....
....
....
....
....

5. What should you do if you notice someone has poor oral hygiene?

....

....

....

....

....

....

6. What are some of the challenges associated with maintaining good oral hygiene in people who have dysphagia and communication disabilities?

....

....

....

....

....

....

....

....

....

....

....

....

....

....

....

7. What are some strategies for overcoming these challenges?

....
....
....
....
....
....
....
....
....
....
....
....
....
....
....
....
....
....
....
....
....
....
....
....
....

Placement activities

The following activities are designed to be completed on placement or when in your new post.

Activity 1: General observation and communication status

Resources

- Armstrong, E. (2003). Communication culture in acute speech pathology settings: Current issues. *International Journal of Speech-Language Pathology, 5*(2), 137–143.
- Costello, J.M. (2000). AAC intervention in the intensive care unit: The Childrens' Hospital Boston model. *Augmentative and Alternative Communication, 16,* 137–153.
- Finke, E., Light, J. & Kitko, L. (2008). A systematic review of the effectiveness of nurse communication with patients with complex needs with a focus on the use of augmentative and alternative communication. *Journal of Clinical Nursing, 17,* 2102–2115.
- Fung, K., Lyden, T., Lee, J., Urba, S., Worden, F. et al. (2005). Voice and swallowing outcomes of an organ-preservation trial for advanced laryngeal cancer. *International Journal of Radiation Oncology Biology Physics, 3(5),* 1395–1399.
- Hemsley, B. & Baladin, S. (2003). Disability, dysphagia, and complex communication needs: Making room for communication in ethical decisions about dysphagia. *International Journal of Speech-Language Pathology, 5(2),* 125–129.

> **Ask your clinical educator or supervisor to select a client for you to do this activity with. Observe the client during a rest period or during a conversation. Use this observation period to understand how the client communicates with others.**
> **Do not offer advice or strategies without first consulting your clinical educator.**

1. Fill out the following form:

(a) Describe the environment in which you are observing the client, i.e. comment on noise level, distracters, and opportunities to communicate.

....
....
....
....
....
....

(b) Comment on the client's level of alertness and responsiveness.

....
....
....
....
....
....

(c) Comment on the posture/position of the client.

....
....
....
....
....
....
....

(d) Comment on their level of activity and mobility.

....

....

....

....

....

....

(e) Comment on whether any of the following are present: a naso-gastric tube; a tracheostomy tube; a gastrostomy tube; an intravenous line; a central line; etc.

....

....

....

....

....

....

....

(f) Comment on respiratory function at rest and during vocalisation/ speech.

....

....

....

....

....

....

....

(g) Comment on level of oral secretion during vocalisation/ conversation and at rest.

....
....
....
....
....
....
....

(h) Comment on whether the client is orientated to time and place.

....
....
....
....
....
....
....

(i) Comment on the client's comprehension ability.

....
....
....
....
....
....
....

(j) Comment on the client's expressive language ability. If the client is an infant or child with complex needs, focus on their non-verbal skills and vocalisations.

....
....
....
....
....
....

(k) Comment on the client's voice quality, intelligibility and vocalisations/speech.

....
....
....
....
....
....

(l) Comment on any augmentative and alternative communication support used. If you are observing the client during a mealtime, then describe how these materials were used to support the client during the mealtime.

....
....
....
....
....
....

(m) Indicate if English is an additional language and if an interpreter was used.

....

....

....

....

....

....

(n) Comment on why it is important to consider your client's communication ability when planning your dysphagia assessment, therapy or management.

....

....

....

....

....

....

....

....

....

....

....

....

....

....

....

....

Activity 2: Mealtime observation

Resources

- McGillivray, T. & Marland, G. (1999). Assisting demented patients with feeding: Problems in a ward environment. A review of the literature. *Journal of Advanced Nursing, 29(3)*, 608–614.
- Steele, C., Greenwood, C., Ens, I., Robertson, C. & Seidman-Carlson, R. (1997). Mealtime difficulties in a home for the aged: Not just dysphagia. *Dysphagia, 12(1)*, 43–50.

1. In this activity, you will observe a client during an entire mealtime. Before starting this activity, ask your clinical educator or supervisor for a client that is suitable for this activity. Before observing your client, ask your clinical educator or supervisor if there are any specific management strategies that the client uses as part of their programme, e.g. swallowing manoeuvres, pacing, dummy spoon presentations, slow flow teats, etc. List these below:

....

....

....

....

....

....

....

....

> **Now you are ready to observe your client during an entire mealtime. Do not offer advice or suggest strategies during this observation**
> **JUST OBSERVE.**

2. Describe any equipment that the client is using during their meal, how this equipment helps them with eating or drinking and whether it is effective.

....

....

....

....

....

....

....

....

....

....

....

....

3. Comment on the client's level of independence and whether they can feed themselves or are fed.

....

....

....

....

....

....

....

....

....

....

4. Comment on the client's posture before the meal.

....
....
....
....
....
....
....

5. Describe the consistency of the food being eaten.

....
....
....
....
....
....
....

6. Comment on the environment in which the client is eating. Is it noisy? What is the lighting like? Is it in a dining room or are they eating alone?

....
....
....
....
....
....
....

7. Comment on the rate at which the client is fed/feeds themselves and the quantity of the bolus.

....

....

....

....

....

....

8. Comment on whether or not the client becomes tired during the meal. If so, describe what happens.

....

....

....

....

....

....

9. Comment on any features occurring that you feel are indicative of risk. **You must inform your clinical educator or supervisor of these risks.**

....

....

....

....

....

....

....

10. Does any communication take place during the meal? For example, between the person feeding the client and the client. Describe the communication that occurs. Remember to also include any non-verbal communication.

....

....

....

....

....

....

....

....

....

....

....

11. Comment on whether the specific management strategies that you listed at the start of this activity were followed. If any were not followed, indicate below why you think they were not followed. **You must inform your clinical educator or supervisor if any were not followed.**

....

....

....

....

....

....

....

12. If you had the opportunity to observe a client who is dependent for feeding, then try to observe the client being fed by one or more different carers/support workers. Were there any differences? If so, what were the differences?

....
....
....
....
....
....
....
....
....
....
....
....

13. From your reading, what are some of the barriers to caregivers' compliance with eating and drinking recommendations?

....
....
....
....
....
....
....
....
....

....
....
....
....
....
....
....
....
....

14. Are there other professionals who are or need to be involved in this case? If yes, who are they and why should they be involved?

....
....
....
....
....
....
....
....
....
....
....
....
....
....
....

Activity 3: Information gathering

Resources

- Gallagher, L. & Naidoo, P. (2009). Prescription drugs and their effects on swallowing. *Dysphagia, 24,* 159–166.
- Harding, C., Smith, C., Harrison, K., Cocks, N. & Vyas, C. (2010). A problem-solving framework for clinicians supervising junior staff working in paediatric dysphagia. *Speech & Language Therapy in Practice, Autumn,* 26–29.
- Hendrix, T. (1993). Art and science of history taking in the patient with difficulty swallowing. *Dysphagia, 8(2),* 69–73.
- Leslie, P., Carding, P. & Wilson, J. (2003). Clinical review: Investigation and management of chronic dysphagia. *British Medical Journal, 326,* 433–436.
- Shipley, K.G. & McAfee, J.G. (2009). *Assessment in speech-language pathology: A resource manual (4th edition).* New York: Delmar Cengage Learning.

Instructions

This task teaches you to gather information before completing an assessment. It comprises of two parts: a role play which you will complete with a peer, and an activity in which you will gather information on an actual client.

1. Role play

Prepare a short case history interview that could be completed with a client, their carer or a member of staff. Write a script for this interview below.

....

....

....

....

....

....

....

....

....

....

....

....

....

....

....

....

....

....

....

....

....

....

2. Gathering information about a client

This task is about gaining appropriate information to help you with your assessment. Part of this involves looking at medical notes, observation, speaking to relevant staff, speaking to the client and/or speaking with the carers.

The information gathered from face-to-face contact can be collected either while observing your clinical educator or supervisor taking a case history or taking the history yourself while your clinical educator or supervisor observes.

> **DO NOT collect a case history without your clinical educator or supervisor present or without the permission of your clinical educator or supervisor.**

Select one client that you have seen today and fill out the following form

(a) Relevant background and social history (pre-natal/birth history, developmental history, biographical, cultural, religious, behavioural, surgical, vocational and leisure information).

....

....

....

....

....

....

....

....

....

....

....

....

(b) Medical history/diagnosis.

....
....
....
....
....
....
....

(c) Nutritional status, e.g. weight and height.

....
....
....
....
....
....
....

(d) Respiratory status.

....
....
....
....
....
....
....
....
....

(e) Cognitive function.

....

....

....

....

....

....

....

(f) Pre-morbid nutritional status, including method of intake.

....

....

....

....

....

....

....

(g) Previous speech and language therapy intervention.

....

....

....

....

....

....

....

....

....

(h) Current form and method of nutrition.

....
....
....
....
....
....

(i) Current communication ability.

....
....
....
....
....
....
....
....
....
....
....
....
....
....
....
....
....

(j) Sensory needs.

....

....

....

....

....

....

....

(k) Prognosis.

....

....

....

....

....

....

....

....

(m) Relevant medications and their method of administration.

....

....

....

....

....

....

....

....

(n) Do a search to find out if the medication the client is on will have any impact on their appetite and/or their oral motor and pharyngeal function. Describe your findings below.

....

....

....

....

....

....

....

(o) Related issues such as gastro-oesophageal disorders, history of current swallowing difficulties and reason for referral.

....

....

....

....

....

....

....

....

....

....

....

....

....

....

Activity 4: Oral motor assessment

Resources

- Harding, C. & Wright, J. (2010). Dysphagia: The challenge of managing eating and drinking difficulties in children and adults who have learning disabilities. *Tizard Learning Disability Review Journal, 15(1),* 4–13.
- Love, R.J. & Webb, W.G. (2001). *Neurology for the speech-language pathologist (4th edition).* Boston: Butterworth-Heinemann.
- Mann, G. & Hankey, G. (2001). Initial clinical and demographic predictors of swallowing impairment following acute stroke. *Dysphagia, 16,* 208–215.
- Ask your clinician for a copy of the departmental oral-motor assessment procedure. Use this procedure for the next two tasks.

An example of an oral-motor assessment can also be found on the DVD in the accompanying book: Cocks, N. & Harding, C. (2012). *Developing Clinical Skills in Dysphagia: A guide for speech and language therapists.* London: J&R Press Ltd.

Instructions

This task teaches you how to carry out an oral-motor assessment. It comprises of two parts: a role play which you will complete with a peer, and an activity in which you will carry out an oral-motor assessment on an actual client.

1. Role play

Spend some time planning how you would carry out an oral-motor assessment with a client in your service. As part of this, you will need to script how you will introduce the tasks, give instructions and talk to your client. It may help to discuss how you would do this with your peer. Record your script below:

....

....

....

....

....

....

....

....

....

....

....

....

....

....

....

....

....

....

....

....

....

....

....

....

....

2. Peer examination

Now try doing an oral-motor assessment on your peer.

(a) Inspect the facial features and symmetry of your peer. Comment on what features you think would be important to observe when first assessing a client.

....

....

....

....

....

....

(b) Inspect the oral cavity of your peer. Comment on secretions, oral hygiene, structure, sensation, etc.

....

....

....

....

....

....

(c) Inspect the oro-pharynx. Comment on the structure observed.

....

....

....

....

....

(d) Carry out an assessment of the following cranial nerves: V, VII, IX, X, and XII on your peer. Comment on any specific features noted.

....

....

....

....

....

....

3. Challenges

With your peer, discuss the challenges of doing an oral-motor assessment with *one* of the following: an infant, an adult with learning disabilities, an adult with dementia, or an adult with severe aphasia.

....

....

....

....

....

....

....

....

....

....

....

....

....

4. Task

Ask your clinical educator or supervisor if you can complete the following task with a client.

> **Students MUST have a clinical educator present when completing this task.**

Record the following:

(a) Write down your client's diagnosis below. Using the diagnosis to guide your hypotheses, predict what types of difficulties they may have with their eating and drinking. Write this prediction below.

....

....

....

....

....

....

....

....

....

....

....

....

....

....

....

....

....

....

(b) Inspect the facial features and symmetry of your client. Comment on any features that you feel are of relevance.

....

....

....

....

....

....

....

(c) Inspect the oral cavity of the client. Comment on secretions, oral hygiene, structure, sensation, etc.

....

....

....

....

....

....

....

....

....

(d) Inspect the oro-pharynx. Comment on the structure observed.

....

....

....

....

....

....

....

(e) Carry out an assessment of the following cranial nerves: V, VII, IX, X, and XII. Comment below on any specific features noted. Also indicate whether you did this task with the compliance of the client, by observation, from case notes or other means (if you indicated 'other', please describe how).

....

....

....

....

....

....

....

....

....

....

....

....

....

....

....

....

....

....

....

....

....

....

....

(f) Before carrying out the next activity, comment on the following:

– Level of alertness

– Airway protection

– Positioning

– Fatigue

– Voice quality

– Impact of environmental setting

....

....

....

....

....

....

....

....

....

....

....

....

....

....

....

....

....

....

(g) Briefly describe below how you might assess the communication skills of your client.

....

....

....

....

....

....

....

....

....

....

....

(h) Describe any challenges you faced with completing an assessment with your client, e.g. the client not understanding instructions.

....

....

....

....

....

....

....

....

....

....

....

(i) If you had the opportunity to do this assessment again, what would you do differently?

....

....

....

....

....

....

....

....

....

....

....

....

Do you think, considering the above points, that your client can attempt an oral trial?

YES ☐   NO ☐

> **DO NOT PROCEED TO ACTIVITY 5 WITHOUT DISCUSSING THIS WITH YOUR CLINICAL EDUCATOR OR SUPERVISOR AND OBTAINING THEIR PERMISSION TO PROCEED.**
> **Students must have their clinical educator present when completing part 2 of Activity 5.**

Activity 5: Oral trial

Resources

- Bours, G., Speyer, R., Lemmens, J., Limburg, M. & De Wit, R. (2009). Bedside screening tests vs. videofluoroscopy or fibreoptic endoscopic evaluation of swallowing to detect dysphagia in patients with neurological disorders: Systematic review. *Journal of Advanced Nursing, 65(3)*, 477–493.

- Leslie, P., Carding, P. & Wilson, J. (2003). Clinical review: Investigation and management of chronic dysphagia. *British Medical Journal, 326*, 433-436.

- Mann, G. & Hankey, G. (2001). Initial clinical and demographic predictors of swallowing impairment following acute stroke. *Dysphagia, 16*, 208–215.

- Rogers, B. & Arvedson, J. (2005). Assessment of infant oral sensorimotor and swallowing function. *Mental Retardation and Developmental Disabilities Research Reviews, 1*, 74–82.

- Suiter, D. & Leder, S. (2008). Clinical utility of the 3-ounce water swallow test. *Dysphagia, 23*, 244–250.

- Suiter, D., Leder, S. & Karas, D. (2009). The 3-ounce water (90cc) water swallow challenge: A screening test for children suspected with oropharyngeal dysphagia. *Otolaryngology-Head and Neck Surgery, 140*, 187–190.

An example of a swallow screen can also be found on the DVD in the accompanying book: Cocks, N. & Harding, C. (2011). *Developing Clinical Skills in Dysphagia: A guide for speech and language therapists.* London: J&R Press Ltd. This activity is comprised of two parts: a student-led task, and a client-focused task.

1. Practice-swallow trial

Ask your peer to sit next to you for a practice-swallow trial. While standing **to the side** of your peer, give them a drink and feel their swallow. Continue to practise at least five times giving them a drink and feeling their swallow at the same time. Ensure you give sufficient time between each drink and do not rush. Repeat the exercise but standing to their other side.

(a) Comment on what you found difficult about this task.

....

....

....

....

....

....

(b) Comment on how you think feeling a swallow would be clinically useful to you.

....

....

....

....

....

....

(c) Ask your clinical educator or supervisor to select a suitable client for you to carry out an oral trial with. Write a plan below for the oral trial. Remember to include: what essential observations you will make; the tasks you will ask the client to carry out in order to determine whether they are safe to have an oral trial; and what consistencies you will trial.

....

....

....

....

....

....

....
....
....
....
....
....

2. Oral trial with a client

> **Students must have their clinical educator present when completing this activity.**

Ask your clinical educator what consistency to trial with your client. Under the guidance of your clinical educator, carry out an oral trial.

(a) What consistency/consistencies did you trial with your client?

....
....
....
....
....
....
....
....
....
....
....
....
....

(b) Comment on anything specific that you observed and/or felt, including unco-ordination, timing, strength, coughing, choking, voice change post swallow, colour change, change in respiratory patterns, etc.

....

....

....

....

....

....

....

....

....

....

(c) Comment on information gained from feeling the client's swallow **or**, if you are working with infants or children, describe how you evaluated swallow function.

....

....

....

....

....

....

....

....

....

....

....

Activity 6:
Clinical documentation –
reporting in the case notes

Resources

UK speech and language therapists and students should consult:

- RCLST (2006). Communicating Quality 3: RCSLTs guidance on best practice in service organisation and provision. London: RCSLT
- Health Professions Council (2007). Standards of Proficiency: Speech and Language Therapists. London: HPC

Australian speech pathologists and students should consult:

- Speech Pathology Australia (2004). Dysphagia General Position Paper. Available on the Speech Pathology Australia web page: http://www.speechpathologyaustralia.org.au

All students should consult their placement guidelines for record keeping. Checklists for clinical documentation and examples of notes are available in the accompanying book: Cocks, N. & Harding, C. (2012). *Developing Clinical Skills in Dysphagia: A guide for speech and language therapists*. London: J&R Press Ltd.

1. Take time to look at three sets of case notes used in your setting. Look specifically at speech and language therapy entries, and study the format used.

(a) Comment below on the amount and type of information included.

....

....

....

....

....

(b) Create a simple checklist of what you feel is essential to include as a guide to help you write case notes.

....

....

....

....

....

....

....

....

....

....

....

....

....

....

....

....

....

....

....

....

....

....

....

....

2. After observing your clinical educator carrying out an assessment or therapy session, or using the information you have gathered from previous activities, write a clinical entry as you would in the case notes in the following space.

....

....

....

....

....

....

....

....

....

....

....

....

....

....

....

....

....

....

....

....

....

....

Activity 7: Management

Resources

- Foley, N., Teasell, R., Salter, K., Kruger, E. & Martino, R. (2008). Dysphagia treatment post stroke: A systemic review of randomised controlled trials. *Age and Ageing, 37*, 258–264.
- Harding, C. (2009). An evaluation of the benefits of non-nutritive sucking for premature infants as described in the literature. *Archives of Disease in Childhood, 94(8)*, 636–640.
- Hewetson, R. & Singh, S. (2009). The lived experience of mothers of children with chronic feeding and/or swallowing difficulties. *Dysphagia, 24*, 322–332.
- Husseyin, A., Calis, A. & Turgut, S. (2003). A randomized control trial of early oral feeding in laryngectomised patients. *Laryngoscope, 113 (6)*, 1076–1079.
- Perry, A., Shaw, M. & Cotton, S. (2003). An evaluation of functional outcomes (speech, swallowing) in patients attending speech pathology after head and neck cancer treatments: Results and analysis at 12 months post intervention. *Journal of Laryngology and Otology, 117(5)*, 368–381.
- Pinnington, L. & Hegarty, J. (2000). Effects of consistent food presentation on oral-motor skill acquisition in children with severe neurological impairment. *Dysphagia, 15*, 213–223.
- Robbins, J., Gensler, G., Hind, J., Logemann, J., Lindbald, A. Brandt, D. et al. (2008). Comparison of 2 interventions for liquid aspiration on pneumonia incidence. *Annals of Internal Medicine, 148*, 509–518.
- Robbins, J., Butler, S.G., Daniels, S.K., Gross, R.D., Langmore, S., Lazarus, C.L. et al. (2008). Swallowing and dysphagia rehabilitation: Translating principles of neural plasticity into clinically oriented evidence. *Journal of Speech, Language, and Hearing Research, 51*, S276–S300.
- Schwartz, S., Corredor, J., Fisher-Medina, J., Cohen, J. & Rabinowitz, S. (2001). Diagnosis and treatment of feeding disorders in children with developmental disabilities. *Pediatrics, 108(3)*, 671–676.

1. Discuss one client who you have seen on this placement with your clinical educator. Take this opportunity to reflect on the rationale underpinning the intervention.

(a) Outline the client's goals, the rationales for these goals, and when the goal will be reviewed in the space below.

....

....

....

....

....

....

....

....

....

....

....

....

....

....

....

....

....

....

....

....

....

....
....
....
....
....
....
....
....
....
....
....
....
....
....
....
....
....
....
....
....
....
....
....
....
....
....
....
....
....

(b) Describe below how you would communicate these goals to a carer, a school team, nursing staff, another speech and language therapist or another professional group relevant to your case.

....
....
....
....
....
....
....
....
....
....
....
....
....
....
....
....
....
....
....
....
....
....
....
....

(c) Are the goals written in a shared multi-disciplinary format? If not, how are the speech and language therapy goals shared with other members of the multi-disciplinary team?

....

....

....

....

....

....

....

....

....

....

(d) List and describe below the dysphagia outcome measures that are used by the team managing the client.

....

....

....

....

....

....

....

....

....

....

....

....

(e) Outline the roles of the other professionals who are involved in managing the client.

....

....

....

....

....

....

....

....

....

....

....

....

....

....

....

....

....

....

....

....

....

....

....

Activity 8: Videofluoroscopic swallowing study (VFSS)

Resources

- De Matteo, C., Matovich, D. & Hjartarson, A. (2005). Comparison of clinical and videofluoroscopic evaluation of children with feeding and swallowing difficulties. *Developmental Medicine and Child Neurology, 47*, 149–157.

- Gramigna, G. (2006). How to perform videofluoroscopic swallowing studies. Available on the GI Motility web page: http://www.nature.com/gimo/contents/pt1/full/gimo95.html

- Gates, J., Hartnell, G. & Gramigna, G. (2007). Videofluoroscopy and swallowing studies for neurologic disease: A primer. *Radiographics, 27*, 583–584.

- Hiorns, M. & Ryan, M. (2006). Current practice in paediatric videofluoroscopy. *Pediatric Radiology, 36*, 911–919.

- Langmore, S. (2003). Evaluation of oropharyngeal dysphagia: Which diagnostic tool is superior? *Current Opinion in Otolaryngology and Head and Neck Surgery, 11(6)*, 485–489.

- Martin-Harris, B., Brodsky, M., Michel, Y., Lee, F. & Walters, B. (2007). Delayed initiation of the pharyngeal swallow: Normal variability in adult swallows. *Journal of Speech, Language, and Hearing Research, 50(3)*, 585–594.

Australian speech pathologists and students should consult:

- Speech Pathology Australia (2005). Dysphagia: Modified Barium Swallow Position Paper. Available on the Speech Pathology Australia web page: http://www.speechpathology australia.org.au

UK speech and language therapists and students should consult:

- RCSLT (2007). Videofluoroscopic Evaluation of Oropharyngeal Swallowing Disorders (VFS) in Adults: The Role of Speech and Language Therapists: Policy Statement. Available on the RCSLT web page: http://www.rcslt.org

> **Before participating in a 'live' videofluoroscopic swallowing study, please consult your university and/or service provider's policy with regards to your own radiation exposure.**

This task will be a part of a tutorial/workshop setting where you will have opportunities to discuss and ask questions about this procedure. You will watch a videofluoroscopic swallowing study (VFSS) either live at your service or on DVD.

VFSS videos are available on the DVD in the accompanying book: Cocks, N. & Harding, C. (2012). *Developing Clinical Skills in Dysphagia: A guide for speech and language therapists.* London: J&R Press Ltd.

1. Watch a videofluoroscopic swallowing study (VFSS).

(a) Were there any signs of dysphagia? If so, what were they?

....

....

....

....

....

....

....

....

....

....

....

....

....

....

....

....

....

....

(b) Comment on the advantages and the disadvantages of the VFSS.

....

....

....

....

....

....

....

....

....

....

....

....

....

....

....

....

....

....

....

....

(c) If you have access to the results of the client's bedside assessment, then comment on how the VFSS findings compare to the outcomes of the bedside assessment. Do the VFSS findings contribute anything new? If yes, describe them below.

....

....

....

....

....

....

....

....

....

....

....

....

....

....

....

....

....

....

....

....

....

....

2. With a peer, script how you would break 'bad news', e.g. the VFSS examination indicates that the client should not eat/feed orally.

....

....

....

....

....

....

....

....

....

....

....

....

....

....

....

....

....

....

....

....

....

....

....

....

....

....

....

Activity 9: Fibreoptic endoscopic evaluation of swallowing (FEES)

Resources

- Aviv, J. (2000). Prospective, randomized outcome study of endoscopy vs. modified barium swallow in patients with dysphagia. *Laryngoscope, 110,* 563–574.

- Hartnick, C., Hartley, B. Miller, C. & Willging, J. (2000). Pediatric fiberoptic endoscopic evaluation of swallowing. *Annals of Otology, Rhinology and Laryngology, 109(11),* 996–999.

- Kelly, A.M., Drinnan, M.J. & Leslie, P. (2007). Assessing penetration and aspiration: How do videofluoroscopy and fiberoptic endoscopic evaluation of swallowing compare? *The Laryngoscope, 117(10),* 1723–1727.

- Langmore, S. (2006). Endoscopic evaluation of oral and pharyngeal phases of swallowing. Available on the GI Motility Online web page at: http://www.nature.com/gimo/contents/pt1 /full/gimo28.html

- Langmore, S., Schatz, K. & Olson, N. (1991). Endoscopic and videofluoroscopic evaluations of swallowing and aspiration. *Annals of Otology, Rhinology and Laryngology, 100,* 678–681.

- Leder, S. (2002). Aspiration risk after acute stroke: Comparison of clinical examination and fiberoptic endoscopic evaluation of swallowing. *Dysphagia, 17,* 214–218.

- Migliore, L., Scoopo, F. & Robey, K. (1999). Fiberoptic examination of swallowing in children and young adults with severe developmental disability. *American Journal of Speech Language Pathology, 8,* 303–308.

- Rao, N., Brady, S., Chaudhuri, G., Donzelli, J. & Wesling, M. (2003). Gold-Standard? Analysis of the videofluoroscopic and fiberoptic endoscopic swallow examinations. *Journal of Applied Research 3,* 1–8.

- Willging, J., Miller, C., Hogan, M. & Rudolph, C. (1996). Fiberoptic endoscopic evaluation of swallowing in children: A preliminary report of 100 procedures. *Dysphagia, 11,* 162.

Australian speech pathologists and students should consult:

- Speech Pathology Australia (2007). Fibreoptic Endoscopic Evaluation of Swallowing Position Paper. Available on the Speech Pathology Australia web page: http://www.speechpathologyaustralia.org.au

UK speech and language therapists and students should consult:

- RCSLT (2009). Fibreoptic Endoscopic Evaluation of Swallowing (FEES): The role of speech and language therapy: Policy Statement. Available on the RCSLT web page: http://www.rcslt.org

> **This task will be part of a tutorial/workshop where you will have opportunities to discuss and ask your clinical educator or supervisor questions about this procedure. Watch a video of a client being assessed with FEES either at your service or from the videos available at the following web page: http://www.nature.com/gimo/contents/pt1 /full/gimo28.html**

1. Watch a FEES.

(a) Were there any signs of dysphagia? If so, what were they?

....

....

....

....

....

....

....

....

....

....

....

....

....

....

....

(b) Comment on the advantages and the disadvantages of using
FEES in assessment.

....

....

....

....

....

....

....

....

....

....

....

....

....

....

....

....

....

....

....

2. When would FEES be unsuitable?

....
....
....
....
....
....
....
....
....
....
....
....
....
....
....
....
....
....
....
....
....
....
....
....

3. Script with a peer how you would break 'bad news', i.e. the FEES examination indicates that the client should not eat/feed orally.

....

....

....

....

....

....

....

....

....

....

....

....

....

....

....

....

....

....

....

....

....

....

....

....

Activity 10: Clinical documentation: Report writing

Resources

- Reports from your clinical setting.
- Kind, A., Anderson, P., Hind, J., Robbins, J. & Smith, M. (2011). Omission of dysphagia therapies in hospital discharge communications, *Dysphagia, 26(1)*, 49–56.

UK students and therapists should check placement, CQ3 and HPC guidelines for guidelines for report writing.

Australian students and therapists should check placement guidelines at Speech Pathology Australia.

Report writing checklists and examples of reports are available in the accompanying book: Cocks, N. & Harding, C. (2012). *Developing Clinical Skills in Dysphagia: A guide for speech and language therapists.* London: J&R Press Ltd.

1. Take time to look at two or three reports used at your clinic or in the accompanying book.

(a) Comment below on the amount and type of information included.

....
....
....
....
....
....
....
....
....

....

....

....

....

....

....

....

....

....

....

....

....

....

(b) Create a simple checklist of what you think is essential to include as a guide to help you write your report.

....

....

....

....

....

....

....

....

....

....

....

....

....

....

....

....

....

....

....

....

....

....

....

....

....

....

....

....

....

....

....

....

....

....

....

....

....

....

....

2. Imagine one of the clients you have seen is being referred to another facility. Using the information you have gathered from previous activities, write a referral report below about your client for a speech and language therapist who will be taking on the care of the client at the other facility.

....

....

....

....

....

....

....

....

....

....

....

....

....

....

....

....

....

....

....

....

....

....

....
....
....
....
....
....
....
....
....
....
....
....
....
....
....
....
....
....
....
....
....
....
....
....
....
....

Activity 11: Thickened fluids

Resources

- Chadwick, D., Jolliffe, J. & Goldbart, J. (2003). Adherence to eating and drinking guidelines for adults with intellectual disabilities and dysphagia. *American Journal on Mental Retardation, 108*, 202–211.

- Cichero, J., Atherton, M., Bellis-Smith, N. & Suter, M. (2007). Texture-modified foods and thickened fluids as used for individuals with dysphagia: Australian standardised labels and definitions. *Nutrition and Dietetics, 64,* S53–S76.

- Dewar, R. & Joyce, M. (2006). Time-dependent rheology of starch thickeners and the clinical implications for dysphagia therapy. *Dysphagia, 21*(4), 264–269.

- Garcia, J., Chambers, E., Matta, Z. & Clark, M. (2005). Serving temperature viscosity measurements of nectar- and honey-thick liquids. *Dysphagia, 23*, 65–75.

- Goulding, R. & Bakheit, A. (2000). Evaluation of the benefits of monitoring fluid thickness in the dietary management of dysphagic stroke patients. *Clinical Rehabilitation, 14*, 119–124.

- Khoshoo, V., Ross, G., Brown, S. & Edell, D. (2000). Smaller volume, thickened formulas in the management of gastroesophageal reflux in thriving infants. *Journal of Pediatric Gastroenterology and Nutrition, 31*, 554–556.

- Robbins, J., Gensler, G., Hind, J., Logemann, J., Lindbald, A., Brandt, D. et al. (2008). Comparison of 2 interventions for liquid aspiration on pneumonia incidence. *Annals of Internal Medicine, 148*, 509–518.

- Rempel, G. & Moussavi, Z. (2005). The effect of viscosity on the breath–swallow pattern of young people with cerebral palsy. *Dysphagia, 20,* 108–112.

- Stuart, S. & Motz, J. (2009). Viscosity in infant dysphagia management: Comparison of viscosity of thickened liquids used in assessment and thickened liquids used in treatment. *Dysphagia, 24*, 412–422.

- Vivanti, A., Campbell, K., Suter, M., Hannan-Jones, M. & Hulcombe, J. (2009). Contribution of thickened drinks, food and enteral and parenteral fluids to fluid intake in hospitalised patients with dysphagia. *Journal of Human Nutrition and Dietetics, 22,* 148–155.

Australian speech pathologists and students should refer to:

- Dietitians Association of Australia and The Speech Pathology Association of Australia Limited (2007). Texture-modified foods and thickened fluids as used for individuals with dysphagia: Australian standardised labels and definitions. *Nutrition & Dietetics, 64,* S53–S76. Available online at: http://onlinelibrary. wiley.com/doi/10.1111/j.1747-0080.2007.00153.x/full

UK speech and language therapists and students should refer to:

- British Dietetic Association (2009). National Descriptors for Texture Modification in Adults. Available on the British Dietetic Association web page at: http://www.bda.uk.com
- Videos about thickened fluids can be found on the DVD in the accompanying book: Cocks, N. & Harding, C. (2012). *Developing Clinical Skills in Dysphagia: A guide for speech and language therapists.* London: J&R Press Ltd.

Useful equipment
- Thickener and drinks to thicken

Instructions

After reading the above articles, answer the questions below.

1. What impacts on the viscosity of thickened fluids?

....

....

....

....

....

....

....

....

....

....

....

2. How accurate are people at making thickened fluids? What could improve their accuracy?

....

....

....

....

....

....

....

....

....

....

....

3. What evidence is there that this is an effective treatment for reducing the risk of aspiration pneumonia?

....

....

....

....

....

....

....
....
....
....
....

4. How does the level of viscosity impact on the effectiveness of this treatment?

....
....
....
....
....
....
....
....
....
....
....

5. What are the side effects of and issues with prescribing thickened fluids?

....
....
....
....
....
....

....

....

....

....

....

5. Ask your clinical educator or supervisor for some thickener. Prepare two thickened drinks of different thickness using the instructions provided by the manufacturer or given to you by your clinical educator or supervisor.

(a) How easy was it to make the thickened fluid? Did your thickened fluid have any lumps in it?

....

....

....

....

....

....

....

....

....

....

....

(b) Now taste your thickened fluid. Describe the taste, texture and sensation.

....

....

....

....
....
....
....
....
....
....
....

6. Think of the social activities that you have attended in the last month. How many of these involved drinking liquids? How would you feel if you had to prepare yourself thickened drinks for all of these occasions?

....
....
....
....
....
....
....
....
....
....
....
....
....
....

Activity 12: Modified diets

Resources

- Cichero, J., Atherton, M., Bellis-Smith, N. & Suter, M. (2007). Texture-modified foods and thickened fluids as used for individuals with dysphagia: Australian standardised labels and definitions. *Nutrition and Dietetics, 64, S53–S76.*
- Penman, J. & Thomson, M. (1998). A review of textured diets developed for the management of dysphagia. *Journal of Human Nutrition and Dietetics,11(1)*, 51–60.

Australian speech pathologists and students should refer to:

- Dietitians Association of Australia and The Speech Pathology Association of Australia Limited (2007). Texture-modified foods and thickened fluids as used for individuals with dysphagia: Australian standardised labels and definitions. *Nutrition & Dietetics, 64:* S53–S76. Available online at: http://onlinelibrary.wiley.com/doi/10.1111/j.1747-0080.2007.00153.x/full

UK speech and language therapists and students should refer to:

- British Dietetic Association (2009). National Descriptors for Texture Modification in Adults. Available on the British Dietetic Association web page at: http://www.bda.uk.com
- Descriptors of different modified diets used by service provider.

Instructions

After reading the above articles and consulting the descriptors of modified diets used by the service provider, answer the following questions.

1. List below the different texture descriptions/modified diets used by the service provider and describe each one.

....
....
....
....
....
....
....
....
....
....
....
....
....
....
....
....
....
....
....
....
....
....
....
....

2. Give examples of food that could be recommended under each of the texture descriptions.

....

....

....

....

....

....

....

....

....

....

....

....

....

....

....

....

....

....

....

....

....

....

....

3. Think about the food that you have eaten over the last 48 hours. In the space below, try to classify it according to the descriptors used in your service.

....

....

....

....

....

....

....

....

....

....

....

....

....

....

....

....

....

....

....

....

....

....

4. Ice-cream should be avoided by clients who have been prescribed thickened fluids because once in the mouth it melts and becomes a thin liquid. Think of other examples of food that require 'special consideration' for clients with dysphagia. List these below and indicate why they require 'special consideration'.

....

....

....

....

....

....

....

....

....

....

....

....

....

....

....

....

....

....

....

....

....

....

....

5. Describe the possible social and emotional impact for both clients and carers of prescribing a modified diet.

....

....

....

....

....

....

....

....

....

....

....

....

....

....

....

....

....

....

....

....

....

....

....

....

....

Activity 13: Working with others

Resources

- Chadwick, D., Jolliffe, J. & Goldbart, J. (2002). Carer knowledge of dysphagia management strategies. *International Journal of Language and Communication Disorders, 37 (3)*, 345–357.
- Chadwick, D., Jolliffe, J. & Goldbart, J. (2003). Adherence to eating and drinking guidelines for adults with intellectual disabilities and dysphagia. *American Journal on Mental Retardation, 108*, 202–211.
- Chadwick, D., Jolliffe, J., Goldbart, J. & Burton, M. (2006). Barriers to caregiver compliance with eating and drinking recommendations for adults with intellectual disabilities and dysphagia. *Journal of Applied Research in Intellectual Disabilities. 19(2),*153–162.
- Cichero, A.Y., Heaton, S. & Bassett, L. (2009). Triaging dysphagia: Nurse screening for dysphagia in an acute hospital. *Journal of Clinical Nursing, 18(11)*, 1649–1659.
- Crawford, H., Leslie, P. & Drinnan, M. (2007). Compliance with dysphagia recommendations by carers of adults with intellectual impairment. *Dysphagia, 22(4)*, 326–334.
- Harding, C. & Halai, V. (2009). Providing dysphagia training for carers of children who have profound and multiple learning disabilities. *British Journal of Developmental Disabilities, 55(1)*, 33–47.
- Silverman, A. (2010). Interdisciplinary care for feeding problems in children. *Nutrition in Clinical Practice, 25(2)*, 160–165.

In many clinical settings the speech and language therapist works in a team. For effective team-working it is essential that you are aware of the roles of each team member. Speech and language therapists are also often involved in training others and so it is essential that you develop skills and resources for training others.

1. Ask your clinical educator or supervisor to arrange for you to talk with another professional about their role in dysphagia management. Comment on your findings below.

....
....
....
....
....
....
....
....
....
....
....
....
....
....
....
....
....
....
....
....
....
....
....
....
....

2. Speech and language therapists often have to provide training about dysphagia to other professionals or carers. Prepare some PowerPoint slides for a training programme in your setting.

3. What did you consider when designing your training programme?

....
....
....
....
....
....
....
....
....
....
....
....
....
....
....
....
....
....
....
....
....

Activity 14: Non-oral feeding

Resources

- Becker, R., Nieczaj, R., Egge, K., Moll, A., Meinhardt, M. & Schulz, R.-J. (2010). Functional dysphagia therapy and PEG treatment in a clinical geriatric setting. *Dysphagia, 26(2)*, 108–116.

- Davis, A.M.G., Bruce, A.S., Mangiaracina, C., Schultz, T. & Hyman, P. (2009). Moving from tube to oral feeding in medically fragile nonverbal toddlers. *Journal of Pediatric Gastroenterology and Nutrition, 49*, 233–236.

- Mahant, S., Friedman, J., Connolly, B., Goia, C. & MacArthur, C. (2009). Tube feeding and quality of life in children with severe neurological impairment. *Archives of Disease in Childhood, 94*, 668–673.

- Royal College of Physicians and British Society of Gastroenterology (2010). *Oral feeding difficulties and dilemmas: A guide to practical care, particularly towards the end of life.* London: Royal College of Physicians of London. Available at: http://bookshop.rcplondon.ac.uk/contents/pub295-ca2ff0c8-85f7-48ee-b857-8fed6ccb2ad7.pdf.

- Sampson, E.L., Candy, B. & Jones, L. (2009). Enteral tube feeding for older people with advanced dementia. *Cochrane Database Systematic Review, 15(2)*. Available online at: http://onlinelibrary.wiley.com/store/mrw_content/cochrane/clsysrev/articles/CD007209/image_n/CD007209_abstract.pdf?v=1&t=gjlj7e1m&s=ea309482962a3f61681b65714b9f11845ea1775f

- Thorne, S., Radford, M. & McCormick, J. (1997). The multiple meanings of long-term gastrostomy in children with severe disability. *Journal of Pediatric Nursing, 12 (2)*, 89–99.

Some clients may have alternative means of gaining nutrition such as tube feeding. It is possible that you may work with the client to evaluate whether some oral intake may be a possibility, or you may be involved in planning an oral care programme. It is still important to observe the client's status during tube feeds as this information may contribute to your treatment plan.

1. Ask your supervisor or clinical educator to select a suitable client who is fed non-orally. You may be able to obtain the following information from the medical notes or you might need to discuss this with the dietitian.

(a) Why is the client fed non-orally?

....
....
....
....
....
....
....
....
....
....
....
....
....
....
....

(b) Describe the type of non-oral feeding your client has, e.g. what sort of tube?

....
....
....
....

....
....
....
....
....
....
....
....
....
....

(c) How often do they receive tube feeds and how much is taken
per feed?

....
....
....
....
....
....
....
....
....
....
....
....
....
....

Dysphagia Placement Checklist

Activity	Date Completed	Comments
Pre-Placement Quiz 1		
Pre-Placement Quiz 2		
Activity 1: General Observation and Communication Status		
Activity 2: Mealtime Observation		
Activity 3: Information Gathering		
Activity 4: Oral Motor Assessment		
Activity 5: Oral Trial		
Activity 6 Case Notes		
Activity 7: Management		
Activity 8: VFSS		
Activity 9: FEES		
Activity 10: Report Writing		
Activity 11: Thickened Fluids		
Activity 12: Modified Diets		
Activity 13: Working with Others		
Activity 14: Non-Oral Feeding		

	Clinical Educator/ Supervisor's Signature